LICK
CATS

CARLI DAVIDSON

HARPER
DESIGN
An Imprint of HarperCollins Publishers

HarperCollins books may be purchased for educational, business,
or sales promotional use. For information please e-mail the Special
Markets Department at SPsales@harpercollins.com.

First published in 2016 by
Harper Design
An Imprint of HarperCollins*Publishers*
195 Broadway
New York, NY 10007
Tel: (212) 207-7000
Fax: (855) 746-6023
harperdesign@harpercollins.com
www.hc.com

Distributed throughout the world by:
HarperCollins*Publishers*
195 Broadway
New York, NY 10007

Library of Congress Control Number: 2016935758
ISBN: 978-0-06-242034-3

Printed and bound in China
First Printing, 2016

To anyone who has ever welcomed a stranger into their home, cat, dog, or human, and given of themselves unconditionally to provide the love that every single creature needs to survive, this book is for you.

Thank you to every animal I've ever had the honor to live with, work with, rescue, photograph, or pet as I'm walking down the street, for providing me so many tiny moments of transcendence.

To the feminist community for giving me insight into the power of being a woman and an artist and showing me examples of success and self-love to combat self-doubt.

To every punk, queer, weirdo, and nerd who has ever felt like the only one who gets us is our pet.

INTRODUCTION

If you ask me, cats are better than us. They can hear sounds too faint for our human ears to pick up, they can see in near darkness, and they have a highly developed sense of smell. They can also climb trees, jump crazy far, and have superhero-like claws that can unsheathe at a moment's notice to scratch the bajeezus out of anything that moves. They are better, faster, and, I have to say, cuter.

However, they are also mysterious. Most cats live indoors—you don't see them tied up outside coffee shops the way you do dogs, or at the park unless they are a stray—and so our experience with our cats is very personal. Anyone who owns a cat knows that they are dignified, smart, graceful animals. They can surreptitiously walk into a room without making a sound, and can hide in some pretty strange and surprisingly small places. It is because of their seemingly constant agility that moments when they do something unexpected, such as missing an epic leap or getting startled by something as inconsequential as a cucumber, throws us off guard and generally comes across as pretty funny.

Lick Cats explores one of these unexpected moments by showcasing a variety of cats all performing a behavior we generally only see dogs do. Each cat was given peanut butter, cream cheese, or baby food and then photographed licking it off their nose or the roof of their mouth. The result was an unexpected glimpse into the humor of the normally stoic cat expression. Tongues darting in and out of their mouths, eyes wide, their expressions fluctuating from joyful to grumpy simply because of how the camera was capturing them. I can say that the cats, even more so than many of the dogs I photographed for *Lick Dogs*, seemed to enjoy the treat.

My cat, Yushi, was the inspiration for this series. She is a constant groomer, licks everything she finds, and continually makes slurping noises that are audible from across the room. She is a stunning black cat who gives off an air of dignity, yet when you spend time with her you immediately realize she is an epic klutz. Toys are reached for with no grace, while flies are hunted, yelled at but never caught. She never stops talking: long loud meows begging for attention, for someone to play with her, and for food. Yushi is a total dork, but she looks like a sleek, elegant mini panther at all times.

I've had Yushi for more than a decade. I walked into the shelter with my husband two days before Halloween in 2004 and we were instantly drawn to her meowing at us from her cage. In hindsight, I wonder if she was talking to us, since that is kind of her thing. She was just a couple of years old at the time, jet-black with huge green eyes. Since the shelter wasn't open for adoptions until Monday morning, we had to wait, impatiently, for two whole days before we could bring her home. Needless to say, the minute she stepped into our house she became a constant fixture in our lives.

Everyday, Yushi greets us at the door with our dog, Saul, demanding our immediate attention, and then claims ownership over one of our laps as soon as we sit down. She wants to be loved by everyone, which is great with our occasional foster dogs, since many of them don't know what to make of cats. She's always quick to assure them that she wants to be their friend. Now, at about fourteen years old, she still wants to play all the time. I really feel cats maintain that sense of play just as much as dogs, and this book helps put that more playful behavior on display.

Many of the cats in this book were living in shelters, such as the Oregon Humane Society here in Portland, during the time of the photo shoot. As shelter cats, they were so happy to get some one-on-one time and some treats. According to the ASPCA, 1.3 million cats are adopted each year from shelters, but more than 1.4 million cats are euthanized because of overpopulation and lack of shelter resources. I urge you to take a pledge to rescue your next cat from a shelter, or if you take in a stray, or acquire a cat in another way, to have them spayed or neutered to help bring that number of euthanized cats down. Many communities also now have feral cat programs, where you can catch strays in your neighborhood either by gaining their trust and getting them in a crate or using something like a Havahart trap, bring them in to get neutered, and re-release them into the feral population to help keep the population down.

Sitting on my couch with my partner, Tim, our dog, Saul, and cat, Yushi, snuggled up together, is how I end most of my days. The waves of appreciation I have for my small mixed species family are often the last thoughts and feelings I have before drifting off to sleep. That moment repeated over and over again almost every day for years has given me a great sense of peace and fulfillment in my life, and I owe the three of them so much for that.

—*Carli Davidson*

Thank you so much to everyone who took the time to come to my studio or welcome me into your animal shelter, and who trusted your cats to my vision. I am endlessly impressed by how the Portland-area community comes together to provide me with such an amazing variety of creatures. None of the cats in this book are "professional models" (but don't let my cat, Yushi, know I said that or she may pee on my favorite sweater).

The following are the cat models by order of appearance:

Lorax Charlie Rescue Tellele Binx Rescue

Carlton Gandalf Earl Grey Gardens Wednesday Marti Big Ben

Rescue   Squishy   Sushi   Yushi   Tim   Plum

Rescue   Quincy   Francis Bacon   Rescue   Diego   Rescue

Abby   Arkham   Rescue   Tom   Jet   Greta

Rescue

Rescue

Maurice

Rescue

Smokey

Rescue

Cal

Rescue

Rescue

Maybel

Smooches

Rescue

Gomesia OEB

Sophia

Dandelion

Frankie

Pepper

Uschi

Murderface

BB-8

Beaker

Malcom

Finnik

Rescue

ACKNOWLEDGMENTS

Another adventure with the seriously crazy cat ladies, the queen of cat whisperers, Tanya Paul, and her almost psychic connection with all felines. Also, of course, Amanda Giese, who reached out to rescues, shelters, and owners where she found most of the cats in these pages, assisted handling them in the studio, and helped build a bridge with the amazing animal adoption megateam at the Oregon Humane Society, which includes Barbara Baugnon and Jennifer Barta. To Amy Sacks at the Pixie Project, thank you for all your support and access to your adorable kittens.

Also thank you to Meghan Murphy for keeping the set running smoothly from nose to tail!

My agent, Jean Sagendorph, another cat lady in my life, who has helped make so many cool projects possible and my editor, Paige Doscher. Thanks again to both of you!

Tim Wiesch, the craziest cat dude of them all, and Yushi's and my favorite human.

To all the women who make art.

To Portland Rock Gym and Sarah Woelfle for keeping me relatively sane in any moment I spent off set this past year by providing me a rock wall, a thin rope, and a reminder of my will to live.

For bringing me endless joy and entertainment: Andi Davidson, Michael Rudin, Joanne Kim, Gio Marcus, Holly Andres, The Durhams, Sierra Hahn, Joseph Russo, Chuck Davidson, Deena Davidson, Jennifer Harris, Dori Johnson, Leslie Davidson, Danielle Davidson, Andrew Davidson, all the Wiesches and kin (Meghan, Marti, Brett, Katie, Maeve, Jake, Billy, Lucas, Eric, Joey, Zack, and Maddy), Joe Preston, Eric Powell, Alana DaFonseca, Danica Anderson, Hukee, Ryan Hill, Carlos Donahue, Janice Moses, Shy Allott, Sarah Grace McCandless, Lance Kreiter, Shane Murphy, Krisi Rose, Seth Casteel, Mike & Bub, the Finks, Erica Diehl, Michelle Borges, Dylan Benadi, Hannah Ingram, Craig Thompson, Scott Harrison, Jen Lin, Marcus and Ro, Stephanie Lundin, Ali Skiba, Glynis Olsen, K-Jo and Veda, Nikon Cameras, the crew at Variable, Pushdot Studios, my team at HarperCollins (Amanda Pelletier, Renata Marchione, Penny Makras, Lynne Yeamans, and Marta Schooler), Gary, Beast, and Jade. Most of all, to the shelters who opened their doors to me out of a place of trust and mutual respect, and to the pet owners who took the time to bring their cats into the studio as models for this book.

Yushi, who never stops meowing, says thanks for taking the time to flip through the pages of this book.